The Good News

by Rosie Bensen

illustrated by Peter Martin

Scott Foresman

Editorial Offices: Glenview, Illinois • New York, New York
Sales Offices: Reading, Massachusetts • Duluth, Georgia
Glenview, Illinois • Carrollton, Texas • Menlo Park, California

Nate Murphy walked dogs at the animal shelter each Tuesday after school. He loved dogs of every size and shape.

He loved shy dogs and bouncy dogs. He loved dogs that knew tricks. He loved dogs that didn't know anything at all.

Nate watched people adopt dogs from the shelter. One family adopted a poodle. Another adopted a basset hound. One man, wheeling a baby carriage, even took home a big mutt. The dog was shaking with misery. But the man spoke gently to it. Next he held out his hand. Then he patted its head. Finally the dog wagged its tail. And the baby cooed.

"This one's a keeper," the man said.

Nate's mom wouldn't let him have a dog.

"Too noisy, too messy, and too wild," she said. "A dog would disturb Grandpa. You know how grumpy he is lately. Your father and I are in agreement. No dogs!"

Mr. Murphy nodded, just as he always did.

Grandpa didn't say anything. He had a look filled with misery. He had been sad ever since he lost his job.

"Nobody in this house understands how much I need a dog," Nate said to himself. "I don't have any brothers or sisters. All I have is a sad grandpa."

One Tuesday Nate walked three dogs.

The first dog was very small. She didn't pull on the leash. She knew how to roll over. But she yapped every step of the way.

"Way too noisy," Nate decided.

The second dog was bigger. He didn't whine. He didn't bark. But he was wild. He whirled and twirled. He chased his tail. He skidded and sent dust flying like a train pulling into a station platform. A dirty station platform!

"Way too wild," Nate decided.

The third dog was the biggest dog Nate had ever seen. When she sat wagging her tail, she swept the platform outside the shelter clean. She did not bark.

When Nate walked her, she picked up a paper bag on the sidewalk. Then she put it in the trash.

"She's just right," Nate decided.

Nate's house was just around the next corner. He and the dog kept walking. When they got to Nate's yard, Grandpa was sitting on the porch. That look of misery was still in his eyes.

Mrs. Murphy opened the door.

"You're taking a longer walk today," she said.

"This is a bigger dog," Nate told her.

The dog picked up some things Nate had left in the yard. Mrs. Murphy looked surprised.

"May I get a glass of water?" Nate asked.

"You may. But leave that dog outside."

"But she's thirsty too," Nate told his mother.

"Well, fine. But don't stay inside long."

Nate took the dog inside.

"Sit," he said.

The dog sat. Mrs. Murphy nodded.

The dog wagged her tail. The floor underneath shone like a mirror. Mrs. Murphy noticed.

"Does she bark a lot?" she asked.

"I don't think so," Nate said.

He let the dog out. Then he ate a muffin.
Suddenly they heard a strange sound.

"What was that?" Mrs. Murphy asked.
"Was it someone coughing?"

"Maybe it's a broken-down car," Nate said.
Nate and his mother looked outside. They saw a
ball fly through the air. The dog jumped up. She
caught the ball.

Then they heard the sound again.

"It is Grandpa. He's laughing," Nate said.

"He hasn't laughed for months," said
Mrs. Murphy.

"Does that dog have a name, Nate?" she asked.

Nate thought of the man who had adopted the mutt.

"Her name could be Keeper," he said.

"I'll be right back," Mrs. Murphy said.

When she came back, Mr. Murphy came too. They looked as if they had something to announce. Nate crossed his fingers.

"Keeper isn't messy or wild or noisy," his mom said. Mr. Murphy nodded.

"And she has made Grandpa laugh again."
Mr. Murphy nodded again.

"Your father and I agree," Mrs. Murphy said.
"Keeper is definitely a keeper! We will let you
adopt her."

Nat whooped. Then he ran outside to tell his
dog the good news.